TEACH YOURSELF TO PLAY

BLUES & BOOGIE PIANO

A Quick and Easy Introduction for Intermediate to Early Advanced Players

BY MICHAEL TARRO

To access audio visit:
www.halleonard.com/mylibrary

1751-5266-1360-7255

ISBN 978-1-5400-0442-0

Visit Hal Leonard Online at
www.halleonard.com

Contact us:
Hal Leonard
7777 West Bluemound Road
Milwaukee, WI 53213
Email: info@halleonard.com

In Europe, contact:
Hal Leonard Europe Limited
42 Wigmore Street
Marylebone, London, W1U 2RN
Email: info@halleonardeurope.com

In Australia, contact:
Hal Leonard Australia Pty. Ltd.
4 Lentara Court
Cheltenham, Victoria, 3192 Australia
Email: info@halleonard.com.au

Speed • Pitch • Balance • Loop

The price of this book includes access to audio tracks online, for download or streaming, using the unique code on the title page. Now including **PLAYBACK+**, a multi-functional audio player that allows you to slow down audio without changing pitch, set loop points, change keys, and pan left or right – available exclusively from Hal Leonard.

Piano	Michael Tarro
Electric Bass	Stephen Toro
Drums & Percussion	John Diguilio & Vinny Pagano
Recording Engineer	Nolan Quartaroli

Recorded at True Music Studios
Smithfield, Rhode Island

Contents

Play-along track: bass & drums only

Introduction

This piano course is intended for the student who has already developed some ability on the piano, and who has an interest in continuing their studies in blues and boogie-woogie style music. The songs and exercises provided are designed for intermediate and beginning advanced levels, with the majority of the arrangements at the intermediate level. The beginning sections proceed slowly – introducing, analyzing, and explaining the fundamental subject matter. This course will progress quickly, as new concepts and techniques are introduced. Audio tracks of the songs, practice tracks, and exercises presented in this publication are available online for streaming or for download. Tracks are listed on the Contents page.

This book focuses on many aspects of blues and boogie piano playing, including a variety of left-hand bass patterns that can be individually selected to produce conventional walking bass lines, or used with your choice of combinations to create innovative bass patterns. Right-hand melodic patterns will also be introduced in numbered order, and may be combined and strategically placed to create complete improvised solos.

Also featured is a section on the popular 12-bar blues progression and its numerous variations, as well as a few unconventional blues varieties. The boogie-woogie style of playing will also be included and demonstrated in several variations.

It is suggested that all the exercises, songs, and techniques be transposed and played in several different keys, to help develop tonal versatility on the piano. The most commonly used keys are C, G, D, F, B♭, and E♭.

A complete understanding of intervals, triads, 6th chords, and 7th chords – as well as the skill to transpose melodies, patterns, and tunes in several keys – is important to develop. It will greatly assist you in the success of this program.

Michael Tarro

Michael Tarro
Author

About the Blues

The blues was created more than 150 years ago. Its origin dates back to pre-Civil War times, when it was used in early slave spiritual songs, as well as work and folk tunes. In the beginning, improvised melodies were used through the telling of stories in song, accompanied by a few simple chords. Over time, this accompaniment became popular and was standardized into a chord progression that became known as the 12-bar blues. Many blues songs utilized this 12-measure format. Later, numerous variations of the 12-bar blues were created and used. Some of these modifications will be discussed and analyzed later, but first let's examine the original 12-bar blues progression.

The 12-bar blues follows a specific combination of chord changes. There are several variations of this progression that will be presented in the next few examples. Below is the most common form of the progression. Each chord change occurs on the first beat of the measure, and extends for a minimum of one measure. The structure of this progression is detailed as follows, shown in the key of C major:

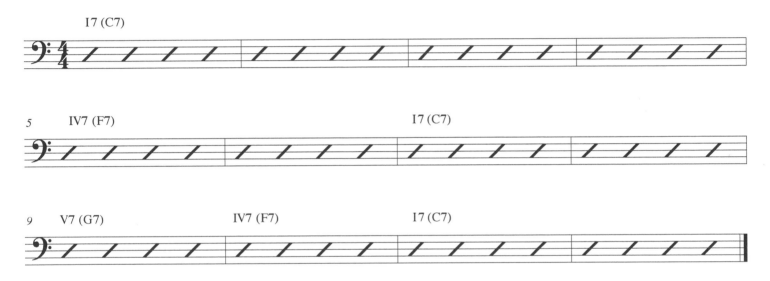

The walking bass line below is commonly used with this progression. It is an excellent practice tool, and an important factor in the development of total independence of the hands. It will be demonstrated on the next few pages.

5

Primer Blues

The following is a step-by-step study focusing on right- and left-hand integration. It is presented in five standard 12-bar blues segments, with the walking bass used throughout the study. The right hand begins with simple whole-note chords, followed by half, quarter, and eighth notes. As the right-hand rhythms grow progressively active, it becomes more challenging to coordinate the hands. Listen to the demonstration on Track 1, then practice this study several times through to achieve a steady tempo.

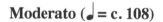

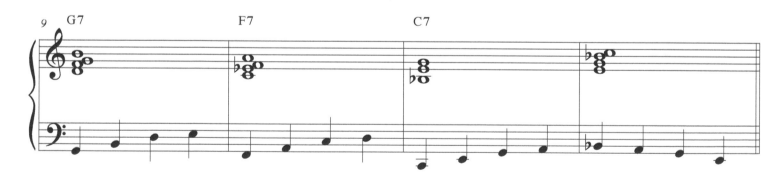

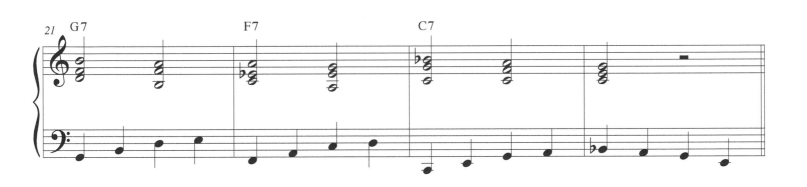

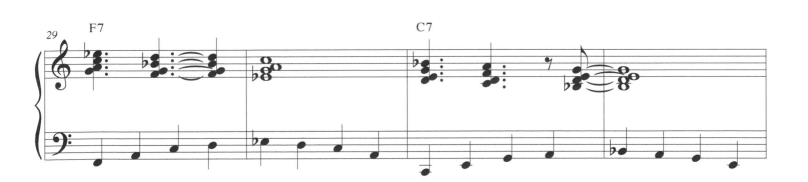

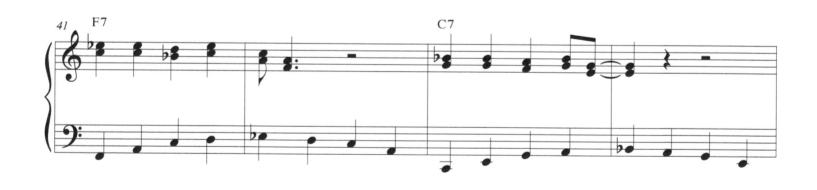

12-Bar Blues Progression
Two-Note, Left-Hand Patterns

Part 1

The repeating 12-measure progression is the framework on which the blues is created. Example 1 is the traditional form, with the left hand alternating intervals of the 5th and 6th. Example 2 produces a slight melodic variation by using the interval of the minor 7th on beat 3 of each measure. Play both examples in several keys to become familiar with all the mechanical challenges associated with key changes. Additional keys: F, B♭, E♭, G.

Example 1

Example 2

12-Bar Blues Progression
Two-Note, Left-Hand Patterns

Part 2

The following examples are variations of the conventional 12-bar blues progression. They are highly recommended alternative forms. Example 3 is the traditional form with the V chord (G7) substituted in place of the I chord in measure 12. This creates the classic turnaround, leading to the top of the progression. Example 4 substitutes a IV chord in place of the I chord in measure 2. This variation produces less repetition, and has a more dramatic effect on the overall progression. The classic turnaround is also used in measure 12.

Example 3

Example 4

First Step Blues

C major

This is the most basic blues tune in this publication. It will help you become familiar with the 12-bar blues progression, chord transitions, and the coordination of playing both hands simultaneously. This song is transposed and notated in three different keys. Listen to the demo track, then try it for yourself.

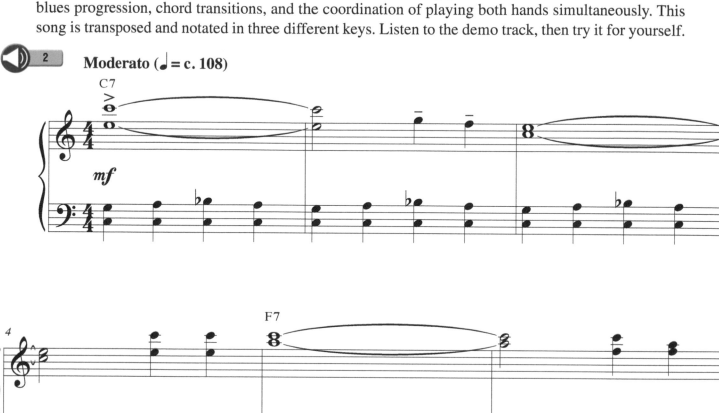

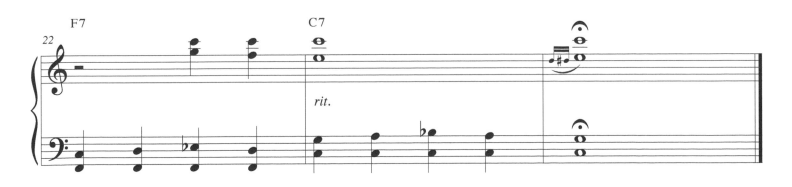

First Step Blues

F major

Moderato (♩ = c. 108)

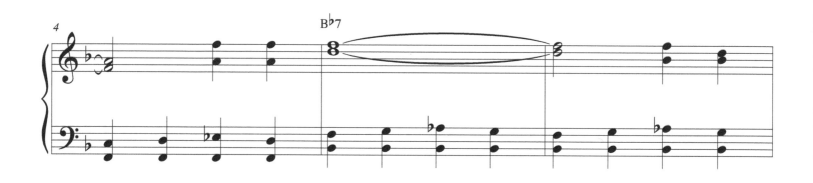

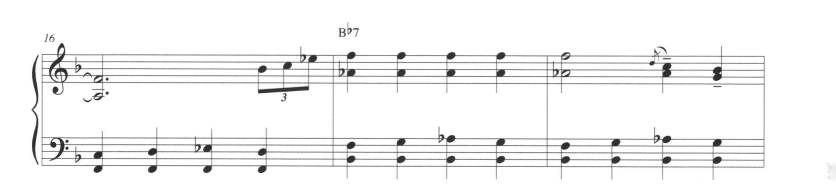

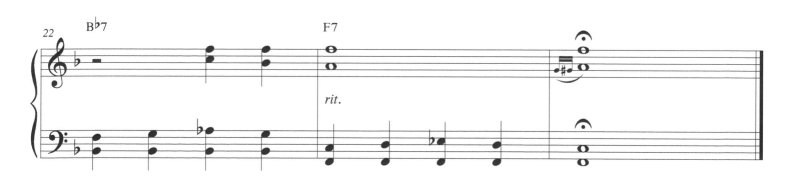

First Step Blues

B♭ major

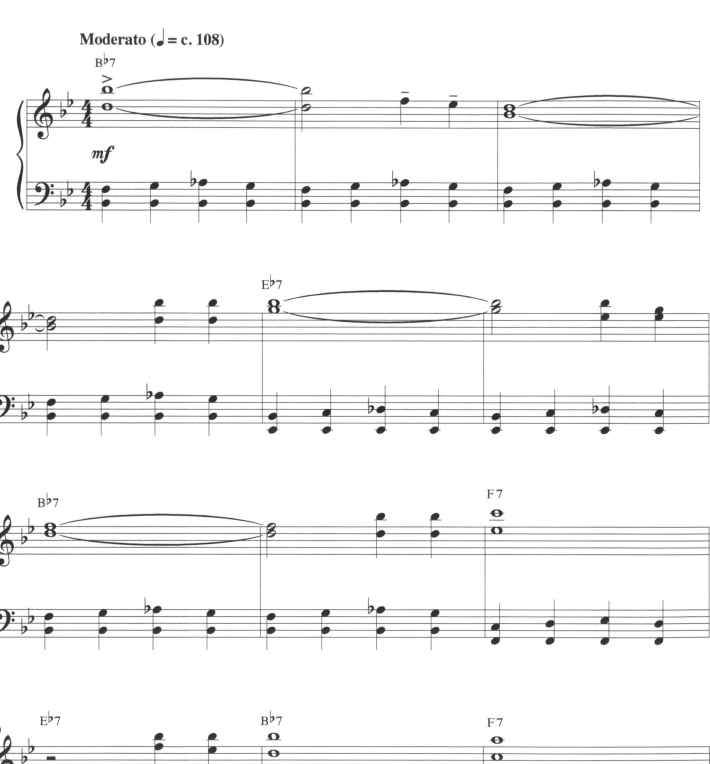

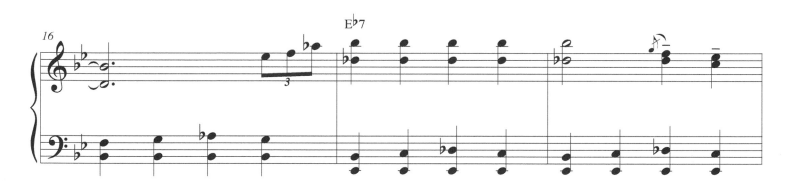

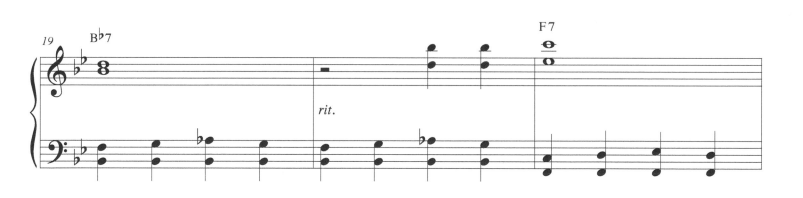

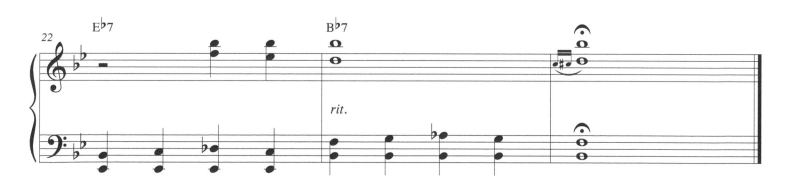

Swing & Dotted Rhythms

Classical notation is based on a four-part subdivision of each beat, or four 16th notes equaling one quarter note. However, the true swing rhythms used in jazz, blues, and boogie have adopted a three-part subdivision of the beat known as the triplet.

In jazz, blues, and boogie music there is usually a notice at the beginning of a song to convert all eighth notes, or dotted-eighth/16th note rhythms, into triplets. This conversion may be stated simply as "Swing," or specifically notated.

The examples below feature two distinct melodies (5a-c and 6a-c) written in three different varieties of rhythms that are interchangeable and frequently encountered in swing music. This notice is displayed above the first measure and will apply to all examples.

Example 5a features a boogie-bass pattern notated in straight-eighth notes. Example 5b is written with dotted-eighth/16th notes in place of the straight-eighth notes. Example 5c is shown in triplets, and is the exact form of notating this pattern. The conversion is not needed when triplet figures are written, however; this type of triplet notation is time consuming to write, cluttered looking, and difficult to read. The alternate rhythmic notations are both practical and more frequently encountered.

Example 6a demonstrates a new bass pattern in quarter- and straight-eighth-note form. Example 6b features the quarter, dotted-eighth/16th-note rhythmic combinations. Example 6c focuses on the eighth-note triplet figures along with quarter notes, representing the exact form of the swing notation.

Turnarounds & Endings

The *turnaround* is a specific chord or chord group that takes place on the final measure of the progression before the form is repeated. The *ending* also occurs on the last measure, but does not repeat. When applied correctly, these techniques create an effective harmonic and rhythmic variation. Examples 8a-d demonstrate how the turnaround may be used as a one-, two-, or three-chord unit. The turnaround chord sequence, when approached chromatically (8b-8d), creates harmonic clarity and strength. The V chord is the solid choice when repeating the progression. Consider the V–I (G–C) progression as the harmonic axis. Examples 9a-d shows how the chromatic approach to the final I (C) chord can also be a useful harmonic tool when ending a blues or boogie tune.

19

Lazy Blues

G major

"Lazy Blues" is a logical continuation to the next level of blues playing. The left hand utilizes the traditional blues accompaniment, while the right hand becomes more stylized with the addition of grace notes and syncopation; this creates additional independence and expression. This song is transposed and notated in two keys to develop tonal versatility.

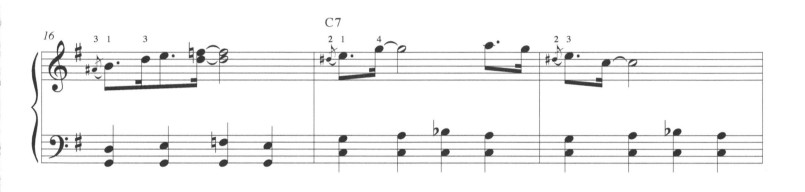

Lazy Blues

B♭ major

Swing (♩ = 100)

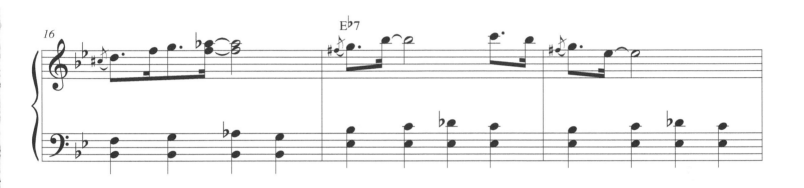

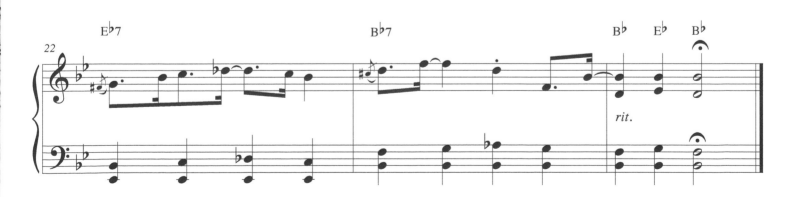

Left-Hand Bass Patterns

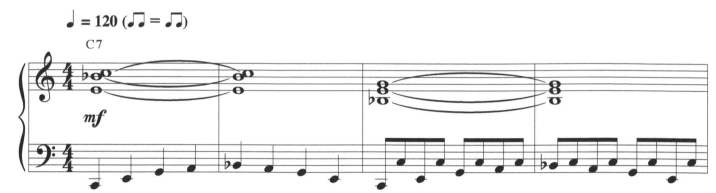

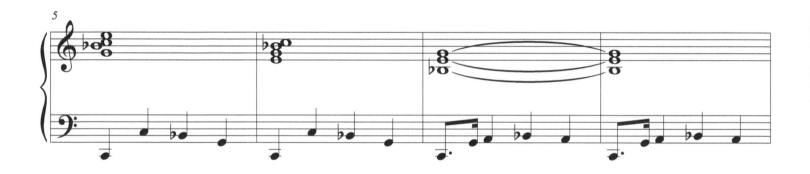

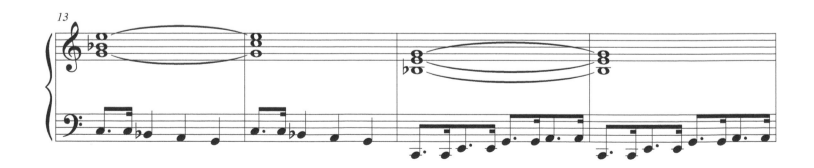

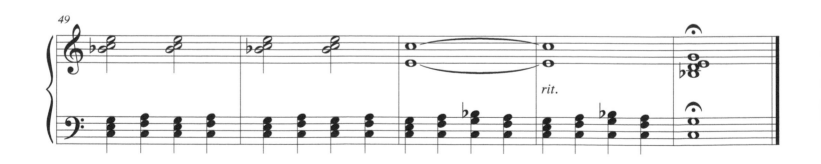

Rocking Bass Pattern

This bass pattern, frequently called the "rocking bass," is useful in a variety of musical styles, including slow boogie, blues, country ballads, and cowboy songs. The notation is sometimes written as straight-eighth notes – or as dotted-eighth/16th-note rhythm figures – and is executed as a three-part subdivided triplet feel. The swing conversion notice is written above Examples 7a and 7b. The complete 12-bar blues progression is written below in two different keys other than C major to assist in the development of multi-key playing and tonal versatility. Example 7a features the key of F major. Example 7b focuses on the key of G major.

Example 7a

Example 7b

27

It's a Cowboy World

This is the first of two songs demonstrating the rocking bass technique. Although it does not adhere to the strict 12-bar blues progression, it is a convincing example of a repeating melodic bass pattern.

The Lonesome Cowboy

"The Lonesome Cowboy" is another variation of the rocking bass pattern, demonstrating a more melodic and rhythmically active hybrid. The syncopated bassline, along with the melodic independence of the chromatic 3rds in the right hand, creates a colorful version of this interesting technique. This variation has less repetition and more sustained tones by the left hand's use of a dotted-quarter note on beat 1 of each measure. An alternate 12-bar blues progression is utilized with the addition of the IV chord in measure 2, substituted in place of the conventional I chord, as shown earlier in Example 4 (page 11).

Performance note: The right-hand *tremolo* in measures 4, 8, and 20 is executed by rapidly alternating the written notes for the duration of their designated time values. Listen to Track 11 for a demonstration.

The Cool Blues

This etude features more independence between the hands. It has a distinct polyphonic texture and an unusual melody. A unique improvised solo is also included. Unexpected anticipations in the arrangement create an exciting rhythmic challenge.

Blues Chord Bliss

Here, we make a departure from the typical blues melody. Although "Blues Chord Bliss" adheres to the strict form of the 12-bar blues progression, the unmistakable chordal texture is evident as the arrangement continues to develop. It contains several jazz elements, such as the use of anticipation chords on the final eighth notes of measures 4, 6, 14, and 16, and a surprise D13 chord lending a final exclamation point at the conclusion of the classic two-measure blues ending.

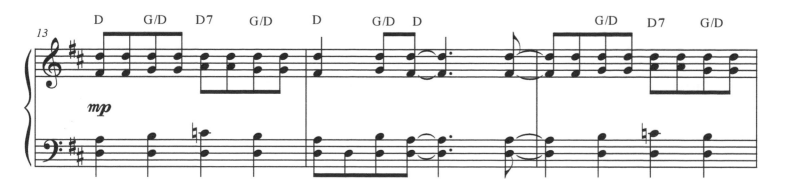

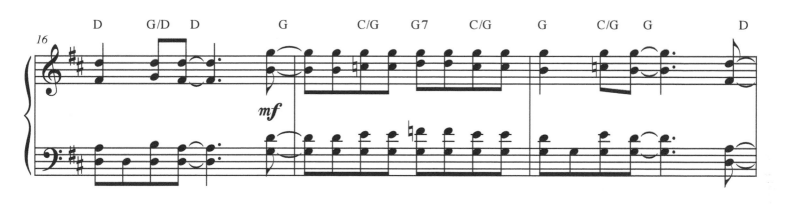

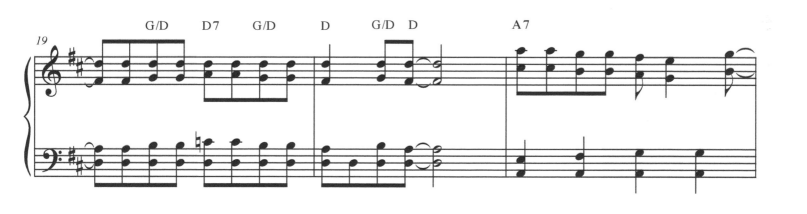

Frankie and Johnny

Considered a traditional blues tune, "Frankie and Johnny" is one of the earliest known songs to use the 12-bar blues progression. It dates back to the middle of the 19th century. This version of the song focuses on a steady left-hand walking bass with chord accompaniment.

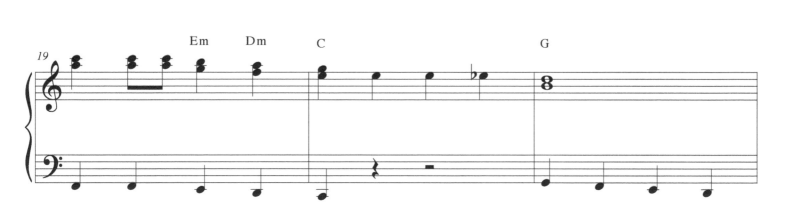

Saint James Infirmary

Joe Primrose's "Saint James Infirmary" is another classic selection, one of the most popular blues tunes ever written. Interestingly enough, it does not conform to the 12-bar blues progression, but instead contains a repeating eight-measure chorus. It is written in a minor key, the exception to most old blues songs written in major keys. This arrangement features flowing left-hand bass patterns; the right hand alternates with single notes and chord melody.

Improvisational Scales

A good understanding of scales and their applications is vital for producing compelling, quality-sounding improvisations. There are four different scales that can easily be applied to blues, boogie, and jazz improvisations. Each is notated below, followed by an improvisational phrase.

Swing ($\quarternote = 110$)

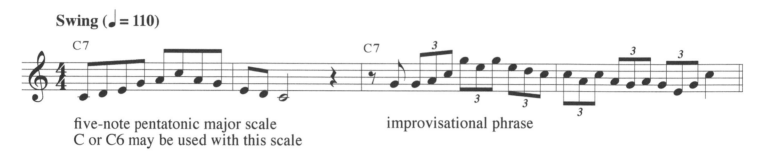

five-note pentatonic major scale
C or C6 may be used with this scale

improvisational phrase

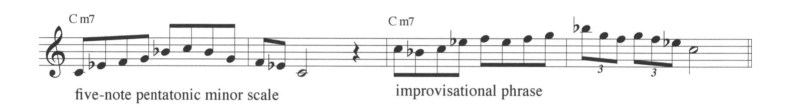

five-note pentatonic minor scale

improvisational phrase

six-note blues scale (♭5)

improvisational phrase

seven-note blues scale – ♭5, ♮3 all inclusive
The major and minor thirds are interchangeable,
and may be played with dominant 7th
or minor 7th chords.

improvisational phrase

Right-Hand Melodic Patterns

The next several pages focus on right-hand improvisational patterns. These two-measure phrases are melodic segments and variations of the previously introduced blues and pentatonic scales. The patterns are individually numbered and include chord symbols above each phrase to help you determine when they are used during the progression. The patterns will be arranged in selected combinations on the next few pages.

pattern 1

pattern 2

pattern 3

pattern 4

pattern 5

pattern 6

pattern 7

pattern 8

pattern 9

pattern 10 (turnaround)

pattern 11

pattern 12 (turnaround)

pattern 13   pattern 14

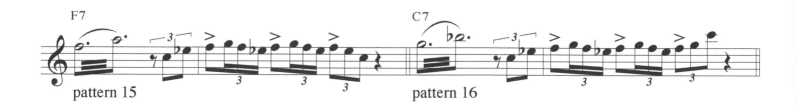

pattern 15   pattern 16

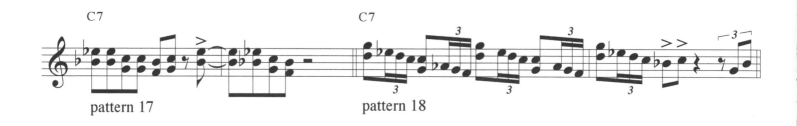

pattern 17   pattern 18

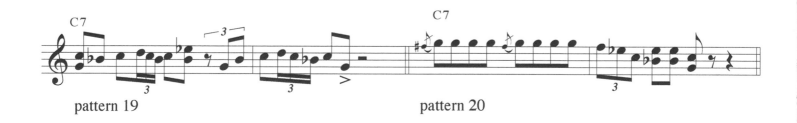

pattern 19   pattern 20

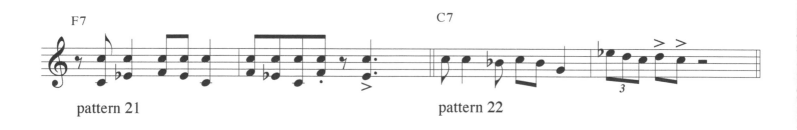

pattern 21   pattern 22

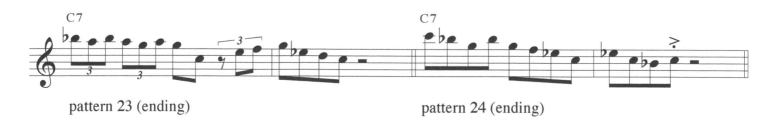

pattern 23 (ending)   pattern 24 (ending)

This page has been left blank intentionally.

Melodic Patterns with Bass

Phrase Combinations, Part 1

Swing ($\quarternote$ = 100)

pattern 1

pattern 2

pattern 8

pattern 9

pattern 10

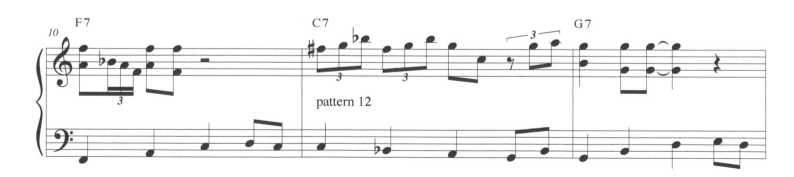

pattern 12

Melodic Patterns with Bass

Phrase Combinations, Part 2

24
Swing ($\boldsymbol{\cdot}$ = 100)

pattern 21 · · · pattern 17

pattern 23 (variation)

pattern 3 · · · pattern 11

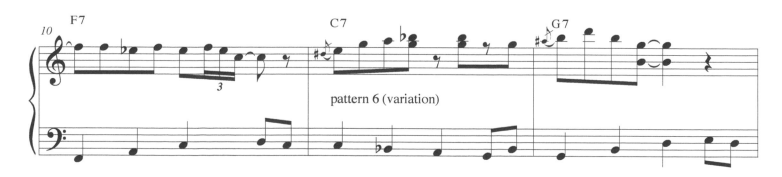

pattern 6 (variation)

pattern 19

pattern 6 (variation)

pattern 8

pattern 16 (variation)

pattern 13

traditional blues ending

About Boogie Woogie

Boogie woogie developed from the blues, becoming very popular in the 1920s. A traditional boogie woogie is a flashy, up-tempo piano showcase built on a blues progression. The strict 12-bar blues pattern is an ideal format for the repeating, driving bass line that characterizes the boogie-woogie style.

The typical boogie consists of several bass patterns, which are repeated throughout the song. These patterns vary melodically, and are based on specific chords used within the overall progression. The right hand is completely independent, and establishes the main theme, followed by an improvised solo.

Not all boogies are the up-tempo variety. A slower-tempo boogie crosses into a musical hybrid some call the "boogie blues." This type of boogie is still considered a showpiece, but without the fast, up-tempo drive. Boogie woogies don't always follow the 12-bar blues chord progression.

Finally, it should be noted that well-executed boogies are superb technical studies, ideal exercises for the development of endurance and complete independence.

The example below demonstrates the broken-octave boogie bass. This left-hand technique is both active and powerful, providing a steady, driving pulse to the rhythm of a song.

Jingle Bells Boogie

This is an up-tempo, fun-loving version of James Pierpont's ever-popular holiday classic. During the verses, the left hand consistently changes between swing octaves and the rocking bass. The right hand moves along with embellished melodic lines and an elaborate re-harmonized chorus.

Bottom Line Boogie

"Bottom Line Boogie" is a fast-paced, swing-eighth-note piece that offers you the challenge of coordinating independent right- and left-hand parts. The right hand, which concentrates on parallel 3rds in various rhythmic combinations, contrasts with the bass clef swing-eighth notes. Practice clean *legato* connections with the right hand when playing parallel intervals. In the second half of the piece, the tremolos present a mechanical challenge while executing a steady left-hand bassline. As always, listen to the demo track before trying it yourself.

52

Camptown Races

Here, this Stephen Foster classic has been arranged in a versatile style boogie bassline that alternates between swing-eighth notes and a quarter-note walk. The right-hand part includes a harmonized melody with syncopated rhythms and an improvisational solo at the second verse.

Perpetual Motion Boogie No. 1

"Perpetual Motion Boogie No. 1" takes its name from the nonstop effect of the melody and the left-hand accompaniment. This version features the traditional quarter-note walking bass.

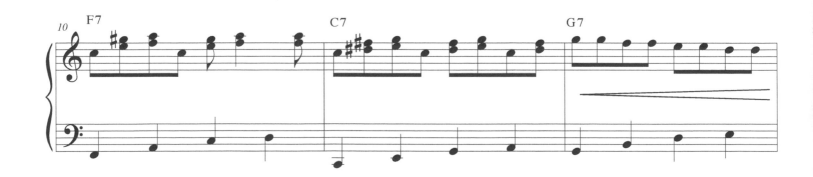

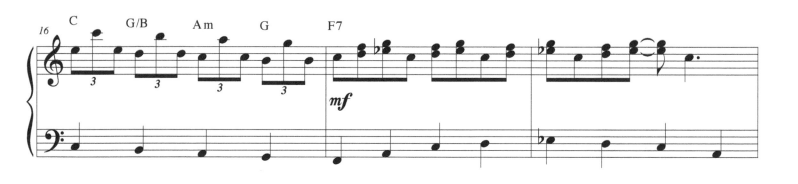

Perpetual Motion Boogie No. 2

This is essentially the same boogie melody and arrangement as the preceding one, except that the bass line consists of swing-eighth notes instead of the quarter-note walk; there's also an improvisational turnaround. This version is more difficult and will require additional practice to master.

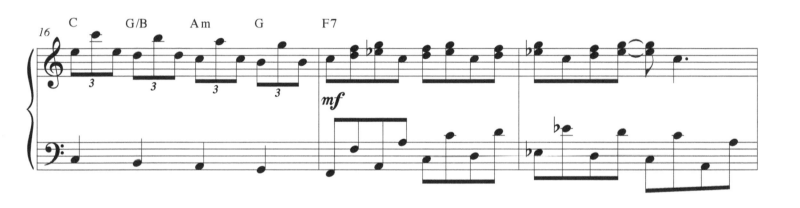

Bill Bailey, Won't You Please Come Home

Hughie Cannon penned this all-time favorite song from the early 1900s. This arrangement uses the final four measures of the tune as an introduction. The first two verses focus on single and two-note harmonized melodies, followed by improvisational phrases through the final two verses. The left hand alternates between boogie octaves, melodic walking bass segments, and diatonic 7th chord accompaniment variations. A *crescendo* chorus tag is used as a dramatic conclusion.

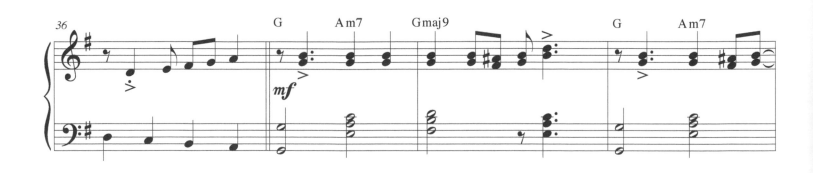

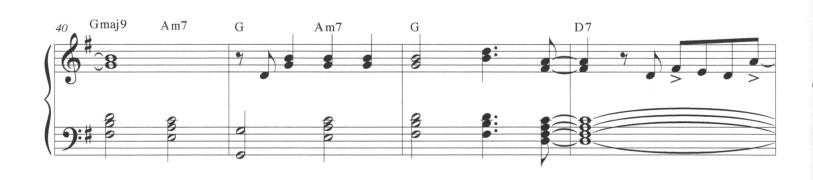

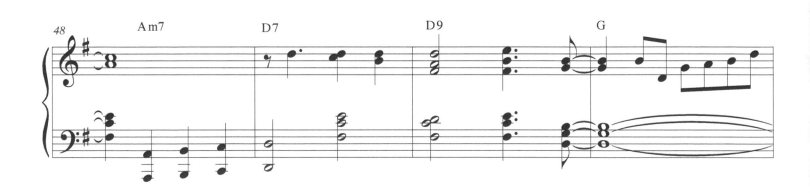

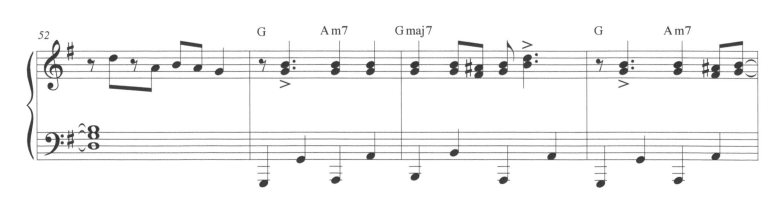

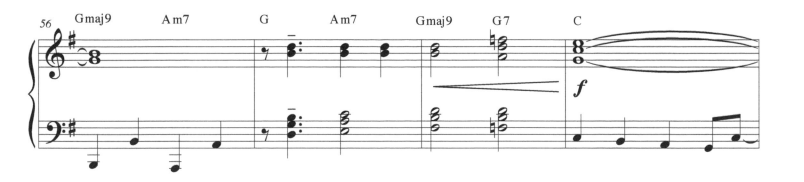

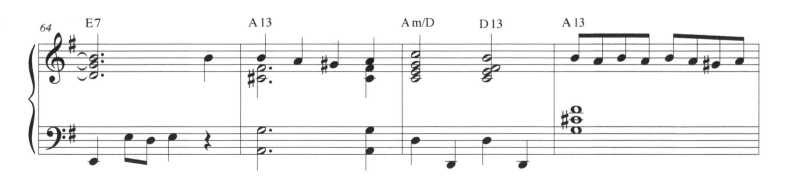

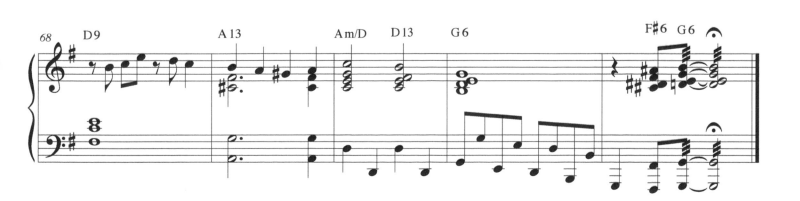

63

ACKNOWLEDGMENTS

I would like to give special thanks to:

- All of my students; for being a true inspiration in the writing of this book.

- My parents; for the opportunity to be involved in music at a young age. Their encouragement and support of my musical training created a deep interest and an eventual direction toward my career in music. This guidance was a true blessing that contributed to my discovering a profound happiness with a future in music.

- My wife Linda; for her love, caring, and endless devotion. I can't thank her enough for her understanding and patience through the years.

- My loving and always helpful son Jimmy; for taking my photograph.

- Ron Montanaro; for his expert contribution of proofreading and editing the original self-published version of this book. It was a great pleasure working with him, and renewing our longtime friendship of many years.

- The exceptional musicians and dear friends who performed on the audio tracks: Stephen Toro, electric bass; John Digiulio and Vinny Pagano, drums and percussion.

- My close friend and gifted engineer, Nolan Quartaroli, and his talented assistant, Sean Boucher, of True Music Studios, Smithfield, Rhode Island.

- You, the reader; I trust you will enjoy the contents herein, and learn to create your own stylistic arrangements. Best of luck in your musical endeavors.

ABOUT THE AUTHOR

Michael Tarro began taking piano lessons at six years old. He studied classical, jazz, and popular piano styles for more than 12 years. As an adolescent, he received numerous awards for piano performances. During his high school years, he supplemented his piano studies by taking courses in harmony, theory, solfège, and counterpoint. He assembled his first working "horn band" and applied his studies in harmony and counterpoint by emulating the styles of *Chicago*, *Tower of Power*, and *Blood, Sweat & Tears*.

Michael continued his musical studies by attending California State University with concentration in composition, harmony, and arranging. He performed in several professional bands while in school and taught piano privately. Upon completing his studies, he returned home to Rhode Island.

Michael has produced commercials for radio and television for more than 20 years. His advertising productions include Doritos, Arlington RV, and Johnson & Wales University – to name a few. He has also arranged various album projects and composed original soundtracks.

His compositions "Schizophrenia Is Better Than Living Alone" and "Alone in Love" received local and national airplay, and were heard on the nationally syndicated radio show, *Dr. Demento*. Michael's "I Won't Be Hangin' with the Guys Again," *Suite for Piano & String Quartet*, and "Old New England" were licensed in the soundtrack of the movie *The Package*. Michael also composed "Prelude in E minor," which was used in the film *In Passing*.

Michael's first publication, *Creative Jazz Piano Arranging* (2010), is currently used for college student competitions by the New York State Education Association. The book continues to be in nationwide demand, and is available online by a number of distributors.

His second publication, an original string quartet arrangement of "Over the Rainbow," was released in 2014 and is performed throughout the USA. In 2016, Michael was the guest pianist with the Ocean State Summer Pops Orchestra, and performed his original composition "Passage of Time," as well as his orchestral arrangement of "Over the Rainbow."